all

is

love

all
is
love

Poems, Essays and Photographs

Book II of the *All Love Trilogy*

Lesley S. King

Copyright © 2019 Lesley S. King

All rights reserved. No part of this publication may be reproduced, distributed or transmitted in any form or by any means, without prior written permission.

ISBN 13: 978-0-9971531-2-5

Inner Adventure Books,
Santa Fe, NM

To Garji,
my one true love

Praise for
all is love

Lesley S. King exemplifies the life of a true devotee, and in *All Is Love* allows us a precious glimpse into her sacred journey of surrender and love. Her willingness to bare all makes her relatable and authentic. This book offers every sincere lover of God an oasis of inspiration and a roadmap to spiritual freedom.
—Jamie Pitts, cofounder and executive vice-president of Great AuPair

This book is an absolute joy to read—simply fabulous! It will touch so many souls on their journey home. It brings spiritual comfort, insight, and focus to our daily trek. Thank you, Lesley S. King, for sharing your divine imagery with the world.
—Rudy Anderson, learning specialist

The challenge for most readers is that poetry tends to be cryptic and hard to follow. Especially the most accomplished poetry often requires tremendous attention and mental interpretation. However, Lesley S. King in *All Is Love* takes a different approach. She endeavors to be a simple channel

while keeping the literary ego in check. Her writing is honest and unpretentious, using metaphors from daily life to pull the reader along in an easy stream of imagery. And yet her poems and essays still have the impact and emotional depth to propel awareness to a broader and more loving vista.
—Amalesh Krien

"I love this book. It was an immense comfort to read it, and a subtle, powerful reminder of what's important in our lives. Lesley's poetry has a wonderfully healing effect, as she shares the truth of her own experience, and how her spiritual discipline has given her strength, courage, and peace."
—Lois Gilbert, author of *River of Summer, Without Mercy, Returning to Taos, and Lost in the Gila*

Acknowledgements

In the past few years my writing has turned a corner. Previously I was happily cruising down the essay lane, when my work surprisingly began veering toward poetry. I've always written poems but never shared them. Now, poems are what mostly come through.

The poetry fits better with my evolving consciousness. No longer do I want to dwell for days in the states evoked in an essay. Poems are lighter, more playful. One can say so much in so little space and time.

And so, my biggest gratitude goes to my spiritual teacher, Sri Gary Olsen of the MasterPath, who constantly reminds me to monitor my attention and only dwell in the state of love.

I also thank those readers who were willing to merge onto this new road with me. I hope you find it as fun and interesting as I do.

My beta readers, Rudy Anderson, Lois Gilbert, Amalesh Krien, and Jamie Pitts, you are all masterful editors and nurturers. Thank you for shining your bright energy onto this project and my life.

Those of you who subscribe to and comment on my blog—infinite gratitude. Your comments are the seedlings that smile up at me after all the planting, fertilizing, and watering are done.

Finally, thanks to my friends and family, who encourage me and love me through darkness, storms, and bright, sunny days.

Table of Contents

Part I

shed your shell – surrender 1

Love Me 2

Homeland 5

The Ferris Wheel 7

Dissolve into Love 9

Shed Your Shell 10

The Freedom of Not Knowing 11

The Relentless Teacher 13

See Clearly through Fresh Glass 15

No Identity but Love 16

The Glorious Saturation 19

The Power of Imagery 20

Loving Beyond the Cliff Edge 23

Part II

the majestic lover – reliance 27

Freedom Disguised 28

Hunting for Love 30

The Majestic Lover 31

My Life is None of My Business 33

What You Imagine Manifests 34

The True Trailblazer 36
The Most Beautiful Pumpkin 38
Transcend Space, Time and Matter 40
The Limitless Life 41
Breaking Trail 44
We Fall So We Can Rise 45
Turn Inward 48
Eden in the Desert 49
What Do You Buy? 51
Thank Your Barbells 52
Re-wild Your Life 53
The Counter Force 54
Warrior Marks 55
Relish the Resistance 57
Monsoon Lovemaking 58
The True Guide 59
Feed the Torrent 61
Remember Me 62
Claim Your Playground 63
Rough Rider 65
Cure the Past 66

Part III

an invitation to fly – transformation 69

Half Moon Dances 70
An Invitation to Fly 71
The Seduction 73
Walk on the Wildflower Side 76
The Call 77
Sweet Intoxication 79
The Clear Road Home 81
Road Tripping into the Higher Worlds 82
The Wrinkle Road 84
Eternal Spring 85
Rogue River 86
The Moon Serenades the Sun 87
Open to All 89
Asteroid of Love 91
Cove of Love 93

Part IV

sail the cosmic seas – 97
We Are Gypsies 98
Hula of Love 99
Sail the Cosmic Seas 100
Born in Winter 102
All I Ever Need to Be 104
Love Hurricane 105

Dance to the Song Within	106
Be	109
United by Our Essence	110
House Built of Kisses	112
The Eternally Bright Day	113
The Mansion Within	115
The Radiant Poppy	117
The Stray Dog	118
Love Eclipses All	120
Time Travel	121

Part V

wag your tail – service	125
The Full Life of a Dew Drop	126
Purrfect Love	127
Love Allows	129
Morning Song	131
Shifting Tides	132
Love with Impunity	133
The Jurassic Scream	135
What If?	137
The Winning Hand	138
Ode to Cilantro	140
Melt into Love	142

Spring Is Here!...143

The Old Lover..144

Invest in Me 146

The True Ruler 148

Become Hopeless...149

My Perfect Teaching...151

Death by Selfie..153

Wag Your Tail 155

About the Author...159

Also by
Lesley S. King

All In for Love, a spiritual adventure

The Baby Pact, a novel

Farm Fresh Journey: Santa Fe Farmer's Market Cookbook, seasonal narrative

King of the Road: Adventures Along New Mexico's Friendly Byways

By the Way: A Guide to New Mexico's 25 Scenic Byways

Frommer's Great Outdoor Guide to Arizona & New Mexico

Frommer's New Mexico, Editions 5–11

New Mexico for Dummies, First Edition

Dream Vacations, Anthologized Essay: "The Native American Trail"

part I
shed your shell – surrender

Love Me

There once was a soul who
loved her life so much
she clutched onto it.

The Beloved said, "Of course,
whatever you want."

And so she held tightly to her house
with its white shutters,
her dog
with his pleading brown eyes,
her work
helping people,
and her parents
who cherished her.

But soon the house needed new windows,
her work became stale
and her dog and parents passed away.

Her heart ached
so that she walked on her knees,
too weary to stand.

The Beloved said,
"When you hold tightly to beauty
you also hold tight to pain.

"Instead, dear one
Love Me...

"Love me like you loved your childhood bicycle
and your cat who ran up the chimney.

"Love me in such a way
that we talk together every moment,
even over little things
like Himalayan salt in the grinder.

"Love me in the shower
and between the sheets,
and as you eat ice cream
or lettuce.

"Love me as you speak with that soul
who sends delicious chills up your spine.

"And that irate neighbor with chapped lips
  who yells at you.

"Caress me as the sea does the shore.

"Shine my light as the moon does the sun's.

"Breathe my breath as the canyon does the wind's.

"Love me and your heart will never ache.

"Love me
and you love your true self."

Homeland

You enter the Soul Protection Program
all the old identities gone,
the torture of being an agent of negativity
finally ceased.

You live in a kind of heaven
a palace below a limitless sky,
where distant blue mountains shimmer
and fat doves drink from a fountain.
Now you work for the team of giving
rather than getting.

You have turned.

The souls you pass in the grocery store
or while walking in the woods,
you live among them but are not of them.
They cannot know of your turning.
They cannot sense your shift in allegiance
from a conspirator of the material
to a servant of the Friend.

And yet you love them
more deeply than ever before
and give to them freely
because now you own nothing
and so have nothing to lose.

You have no fear of being **"made"**
for you are now completely protected
and you know that in truth
there is no enemy,
no other side.

All delivers you
to this place
of pure freedom
in the
One.

The Ferris Wheel

I thumb through the photo album.
There I am in at age seven
wearing a Sunday plaid suit.
Defiant, I dart my tongue at the camera.

In high school,
a pudgy face and body
from boarding school starch,
I slouch in the Y of a tree.

In college, I fondle a Coors,
my favorite companion then.
Morning headaches
cloud my studies.

Graduate school, messy hair, haunted eyes,
first real awareness of life's harshness.
I pretend to be an intellectual,
armored against pain.

A college writing professor
round glasses, tired smile
and a look of desperation
from reading too many student essays.

A travel writer,
I wear a backpack
and stand on the edge of the Grand Canyon,
happy, exhausted, seeking love.

Each stage of life a new incarnation,
new faces, new houses, new towns,
but the lessons remain the same
as I churn on the Ferris wheel
drilling deeper, closer, to the true self.

I see my resilience, enduring,
shining through experience after experience,
a steady presence amidst the chimera of this life,
which mirrors my eternal adventure.

As the wheel slows
the Beloved hands me an escape map.
The next time my feet skim the concrete,
I step off.

Dissolve into Love

The earthly details
dissolve
into
the radiance of love.

Shed Your Shell

Oh, hermit crab with no permanent home,
you live the truth:
that we inhabit shell after shell
only as a means
to realize our true identity.

You shed your home so readily.
As you grow, you take up
an abandoned snail
or conch abode.

Only the Eternal One can ease my grip
on this temporary flesh-and-blood house.
Only that Power can reveal
the immortal love that I am.

The Freedom of Not Knowing

"I don't know."
Words like aspirin
stuck in the throat.

But I try them out
roll them around on my tongue
until suddenly
they turn to chocolate ice cream!

The more I say them
the more I soar.
"I don't know.
I don't know."

I don't know
what's best for me
or for you.

When I can't say them
I am bound
by the straightjacket
of my will.

Saying "I don't know,"
I drop to my Beloved's feet
because in those words
I'm confirming:
Only You do.

The Relentless Teacher

On a moonless night
it seems they harm me
that mate
sister
brother
mother
father
friend
neighbor
stranger.

With a look
a word
a finger
a fist—
slayed.

But the Blessed One reveals,
no thing,
no one can.

Soul in its glory
is impervious as the sky.

Only I,
through what I hold dear,
create pain.

This relentless teacher shows
where my love
must go:
Inward.

And then the hurt dissipates
like winter breath,
leaving me clear
and empowered,
with the sun
warm on my cheeks.

See Clearly through Fresh Glass

The mind wants to build on the old structure.
But the Beloved says,
"Don't glaze this sparkling window into a worn-out frame.
Leave all and start anew."

This requires some destruction.
Pain sparks in the chest
and rips through muscle and bone
but only as long as we resist.

See clearly through fresh glass.
All transforms when we surrender the old
to live the new.

No Identity but Love

I say goodbye to a doll
who wears a cotton dress
and a pine-green coat
her hair cut in one spot down to the roots,
my eight-year-old attempt at being a hairdresser.

I also wave farewell to the teddy bear
I used to hold in the night.
He once played music
but for some fifty years has been silent.

I see them disappearing into the distance
hand-in-hand like Pooh and Christopher Robin.

For years these toys have lived
the way memories do
shut inside a cabinet,
their presence unquestioned.

But one day I looked inside and saw
their journey was no longer with me.

I am not that girl,
youngest of three,
not the littlest one,
the temper-tantrum kid,
the good girl,
the mediator.

I'm also not...
the woman
without a child
but with a dog,
the daughter
the sister
mate
athlete
writer.

All of these, and their memories
accompany the doll and bear
as they disappear down a country road.

In this moment
I play naked
in the luminous poppy field
with my Hero.

No memory but now
no identity but love.

The Glorious Saturation

When the rain pours down
onto my shoulders and hair
I run for cover.
But in this desert, there is no shelter
except for a scrawny piñon or juniper tree.

I have no choice but to let the rain drench
my t-shirt and shorts, soak into my skin
and my very bones.

I slow my pace and suddenly sense
the glory of this saturation.
The drops cool my skin
and settle my heart.

With this immersion, the Blessed One
nourishes my inner garden.

The Power of Imagery

On an icy winter day, I step out of the bank and stop in my tracks. There in front of me shuffles my mother. I see her glossy, silver hair, red wool coat and body hunched over a walker. My heart thuds in my chest. It's an apparition, a ghost!

My mother passed away more than a year ago.

I'm performing the last personal task linked to her life—closing out her safe-deposit box. I have postponed this because in the box are more memories—her antique jewelry, my deceased sister's Navy flight wings, and some silver cutlery. When my mother first passed, my brother and I quickly perused these items, then locked the box away. But if I don't take the contents home today I will pay another year's rent.

Weighing on my shoulder, the bag holds these once-upon-a-time treasures. So far, I have been steady through the process of signing the forms, entering the vault and transferring the goods to a large purse. But now...

As I follow the woman down the steps, a frigid wind whips across my cheeks. She's alive! My mind exclaims, as my heart floods with pain of missing her.

The woman turns, revealing an angular jaw and prominent nose. Clearly, she is not my mother. My heart settles, though with a bit of disappointment. I come alongside her and say, "You remind me of my mother."

She laughs, "At least you didn't say I remind you of your grandmother."

"No. My mother had your same silvery hair and red coat, and the same air of elegance."

She beams. "You just made my day!"

I smile, as tears well in my eyes. I escape, striding fast along the sidewalk to the parking lot, where I climb in my car and close the door before the waterfall starts. I sob from deep in my belly, a weeping that feels good, cathartic. All the while I hold the Compassionate One's hand.

These are just emotions, I tell myself, and that soothes me. I can let them wash over me. As the crying abates and I calm down, I see what a set up this was.

The Beloved knew I would try to shrug off the emotional part of this duty; I would deny any feelings, when really, though simple, the task has many layers. And so, I got to remember walking behind the beautiful soul I was graced to enjoy for a half century. Thus, I am able to wash away yet more of the feelings of loss.

Once home, I make my way through the box's contents. It's a similar experience to seeing the illusion of my mother on the street. Each item is a whole universe. A sapphire ring conjures the Christmas morning my stepfather presented it to my mom, and a whole rush of feelings of anticipation and delight as the ten-year-old me watched. My sister's gold Naval wings conjure the day in Florida when she had completed her training as a jet pilot and received them in a ceremony, which our whole family attended. I was a twenty-one-year-old awash with feelings of happiness and jealousy.

With each item, I observe the images and feelings that arise. Each image is a moment poised on the brink. It can take me down or up. When I'm awake, I have a choice; I can dive down into the universe of memories and wallow, or I can stay in the love and watch the images pass. Today I choose to stay in the fresh ambrosia of the pure now, and I easily make my way through the box.

I have this choice with every experience that arises in my days. I choose either the dead or the live view. The sorrow or the joy.

The loving Image takes me home.

Loving Beyond the Cliff Edge

We ride horses across the plains,
the air bittersweet with sage and sunflowers.
I tie my bay to a ponderosa,
as my brother, sister-in-law, and niece secure their horses.

We hike to a cliff overlooking Coyote Creek,
a pooling oasis that trickles down from the Turkey Mountains.

My brother hands me the box, pale blue with a white dove on the side.
Inside I find a plastic bag, which I remove and hold in my palm.

Suddenly all the ways I held my mother flash before me.

I held her arthritic hand, the bones sharp against my skin.
I hugged her, pressed my fingers into the tender spot between her shoulder blades.

I supported her as she walked with tortured knees,
her weight on my shoulder.
I lifted her off her bedroom floor after she fell, her
arms like liquid.

But I never held her as dust.
The realization that this smoky matter is her body
ricochets through my chest.
This is my mother, my mind beseeches.

But no, the Beloved answers.
She soars in formless grace,
while this is but another piñon shell
scattered across the forest floor.

I step to the cliff edge and sprinkle the ashes.
They take flight, swirling in the wind,
becoming one with her favorite place.

My brother and sister-in-law release the rest
and then, teary-eyed, we hug.
I sense how we are all perched between this now and
eternity,
between these mortal bodies and our everlasting
selves.
And that is our truest task,
to know how much we dance and play and love
beyond this cliff edge.

We ride back, the sun warming our cheeks
and glinting off the gramma grass.
Then we feast, and laugh, and become so tired
we have no choice but to lie down in the Beloved's
arms
and sleep.

part II
the majestic lover – reliance

Freedom Disguised

A challenge is really
increased freedom
dressed in a Halloween costume.

Sure, it has the witch's warts
bat's fangs and
ghoul's claws.

But really, under the wig and cape
we find Divine Love.
It coaxes, encourages,
presses us onward,
pleading for us to surrender,
to give up the darkness of life's graveyard,
to release the passions
like those mini Snickers bars
we hold tightly.

"Open your hand," the Supreme says,
so you can pull it from the jar."

Alas, those "confections" only leave us
with a pained stomach,
a racing mind
and an empty heart.

"Love Me," He says.
The moment we do
the costume melts
like the Wicked Witch
into a puddle,
while we soar free,
airy as a new day
high above the dual worlds
to the land where the sun
always shines.

Hunting for Love

Not this mushroom.
Not that mushroom.
Not this.
Not that.

We come upon a spring
mossy, trickling,
draped violet blossoms
and a clear pool.
Nothing matters
but this transcendent
Beauty.

Suddenly
the desired mushroom—
the Boletus—
appears.

The Majestic Lover

Oh, Unutterable Utterance,
Unrepeatable Repetition
when my heart drops down to my gut
and they mate in their pain,
how I long for You.

As night closes in
and cold hardens the leaves,
the lower lovers entwine.
Dungeon doors clang shut
as they couple on dank cement
with only a simple grate
opening upon a black sky.

The lovers tremble
in the darkness
feeding on the dead:
family losses, parched dreams
mates that came and went.
These are the sighs and groans
of the frozen world.

No longer able to bear the icy copulation
I call out Beloved! Beloved!
And in my single eye, behold the image,
Radiant, smiling
as though nothing could ever matter
in this subzero realm.

The melting happens fast
a softening in heart and gut
as the lower lovers break apart
panting, breathless
spent from their twisted union.

Blossoms form and open,
leaves sprout from branches
like time-lapse video
as I marry the Sound.
The true lovemaking
opens to eternity
revealing the Majestic Lover
that I am.

My Life is None of My Business

Sure, I do my work
clean the house
love friends and family,
everyone else too
and especially my Beloved.

I feed my cat
eat lots of vegetables
and, above all,
do my spiritual practice.
Beyond that, my life is none of my business.

All is in the hands of the Divine.

What You Imagine Manifests

We lounge in a meadow
near a cheerful brook
a lone cloud inching
across a sapphire sky.

It has a head, my friend says
pointing to the cloud.
Yes, I say, as I see
the canine snout protrude
and a curve form along the jaw.

There's an eye!
The pinhole opens.
And tail!
A wisp wags against the blue.

As we speak
the image appears—
what we imagine
manifests.

An exuberant dog
races across the open sky
its legs reaching forward,
a vital lesson imparted
through shifting, flowing white:
We are the creators.

Here in this meadow
where I lie on soft grass
the crucial message:
When I image
the Friend
I realize the Love
that I am.

The True Trailblazer

The trail I have trekked
for countless lifetimes
has washed away.
The monsoon rain flooded
and gushed through
my inner canyon,
dislodged heavy logs
and gnarly brush
obliterated the cairns,
all my carefully carved ways.

Now I tread the streambed
with You,
hop from sandbar to sandbar
climb over flotsam of my past
as You guide me up the canyon.

Within these shadowed walls
I see no path,
and so I must rely completely
on You.
Each time I try to think,
to find a new track
I become lost.

Only You are my Trailblazer.
Only You know the way.
And so I simply follow
keeping Your presence always in sight.

We make our way home
on the true path
that You reveal
in every now.

The Most Beautiful Pumpkin

In the patch I find
the most beautiful pumpkin.
Shaped like a compressed heart,
it is symmetrical
and orange as a desert sunset.

I will give it to my lover.
He will put it on his table
and be joyous at its splendor.

I search and search
for one as enchanting for myself
but only find a crooked pumpkin
taller, with less sheen.

I give the exquisite one to my lover
and he is grateful.

The next day he calls.
"I am cooking pumpkin!"
he exclaims.

My heart sinks
as I attempt to match
his enthusiasm.
I wonder,
Should I have kept
the prize for myself?
Is that my lesson?

I ask the Blessed One.

A rush of elation fills me
buoyant, limitless love.
A thousand butterflies
take flight
as that power says,
"*Here,* inside, is the Beauty."

Transcend Space, Time and Matter

When I'm here
feet firmly planted on the ground
scent of piñon smoke in the winter air,
I transcend space.

When I'm in the now
heart beating in my chest
sun warm against my cheeks,
I transcend time.

When I'm with the Omnipresence,
His image radiant in my eye
a smile sweet on my lips
no *thing* matters.

Freedom.

The Limitless Life

I make a budget:
Coaching fees,
book sales,
rental payments
will come.

Groceries,
utilities,
mortgage payments
will go.

All computes well.
Income covers outflow.

I'm safe.

But what if
I get
sick
sued
flooded
broken
lost?

Emotions flutter in my chest.
Mind cannot compute.

It has no safety net
for the unexpected—
"the reality"—of life.

This is a perfect setup
by God.
Nowhere to rely
but on the unseen.

So I suspend my attention
and image the Beloved.

Quiet comes,
peace in realizing
my eternal sustenance,
the true me.

No budget needed here
For this Power is

Limitless.

Breaking Trail

Though the path is hidden
I hike it home.

Every step an exercise
in trust.

The deeper the snow
the more I rely
on the true Guide.

We Fall So We Can Rise

On a cloudy autumn day, I pedal my bike along a ridge to a hilltop strewn with piñon trees, distant mountains visible in every direction. Elation overflows within me.

I turn my bike downhill on a crazy-fun romp. I bank turns, skirt around trees and grind though gravel patches. A broad smile stretches across my face.

A dark thought enters my head—it has to do with my neighbor. After years of fiery conflict with her, I have found peace, only to feel a cinder rekindle this week. I recognize the negativity and think, *I must chant my mantra or I'll crash.*

Suddenly my tire jumps off the trail and hits a dead branch. I fly over the handlebars onto my head and roll to a stop. Dazed, with searing pain in my neck and shoulder, I call on the Friend, stand and try to walk. With one hand I pull my bike off the trail. Then I sit on a bank of stones.

My hands tingle—a sign of shock, so I put my head between my knees and breathe deeply. I'm miles from home, and at this hour—mid-afternoon on a cloudy weekday—the trails are empty of riders.

I do have my cell phone, and I reach to pull it from my pack, but my hands won't move. They're numb—drawing inward, into cold little fists. I have no idea what's going on, but it feels terrifying. For years I have ridden my bike hard and fast, with an arrogant belief that I wouldn't fall, wouldn't hurt myself. But now, sitting here alone, I see how vulnerable this body is, how easily it can be harmed. I feel its mortality.

I breathe deeply and again call on the Friend. I chant my mantra and focus on the eternal presence. Always these days when I do this, a smile forms on my face, and even now I feel my lips curl up at the edges. I can hardly believe the peace and euphoria that flow in, a glistening calm and glowing love. I sense the truth: that I am not this body that is having this experience. Instead I am a soaring soul, eternal, omnipotent, unfazed. I sit in this state for a while, knowing that I must let the Beloved fix this, for I cannot.

A Biblical verse flows in: "On Thee shall I wait all day."

A cool breeze blows across my back, and birds chirp in the trees around me. Slowly my hands loosen. I remain calm even with the pain in my neck and shoulder. I lift my head and see my bike lying on its side covered in dirt. Tentatively I stand, find my footing and lift my bike. I assume I will walk it home, but after a hundred yards I climb on. Gingerly I steer down the trail.

When I arrive home, I ask for guidance about treatment for my injury. My shoulder hurts when I move my arm, but I *can* move my arm, so it appears as though nothing serious happened. I go about my evening, and during the next few days have an acupuncture treatment, ice the soreness, rub lavender oil on it and swim to keep the circulation going. With the Beloved I revise my feelings toward my neighbor so that once again I see her as a beautiful soul working through her tendencies, just as I am.

But what stays with me is the feeling I had while sitting on that pile of rocks with my head between my knees, an elated knowing that I am more than this physical body, and I can access love even in the midst of pain and fear.

The day before this crash, while wandering through the Santa Fe Farmers Market shopping and shooting photos of squash, apples and chile, I "accidentally" shot a selfie—a surprising image of what looks like my astral being, a truer version of me: lighter, brighter, unmoved by the dual workings of the material world.

If I ride a bike I will fall; if I have relationships, my heart will hurt; if I live in a physical body, it will die; but my soul never, ever wavers. It is steady, immortal, eternal.

It is love.

Turn Inward

When storm clouds darken the west,
turn around.
A rainbow blooms to the east.

When dawn blazes scarlet,
turn around.
Pink feathers the sky.

When a tear drips down your cheek,
turn inward.
A compassionate heart expands and
fills the Universe
with love.

Eden in the Desert

In this desert
where even the most sensuous kiss
dries to a crisp,
where the greatest artwork
blows away in a dust devil,
where even a tear sears to nothingness
in the relentless whirling of time,
I call out to You.

With a heart desiccated
as that giant saguaro corpse laid out
black and eaten on the ground,
I beg for even one green blade of grass.

I awaken, transported,
the howling wind quiet
the dust settled.
Spring green carpets the ground,
ocotillo emits leaves so succulent
you could eat them.
A curved-bill thrasher whistles her glee.

My heart soaks in the dew
the music
the bright warm sun
and knows
this Eden in the desert
is my true home.

Then I see, it is for me:
the pain of those prickly pear thorns,
the burning heat,
the sand that thwarts my steps,
here for me to let go
so that I can know:
All is **love.**

What Do You Buy?

Your friend gives you money
to buy coffee at the store.
Do you buy chocolate for yourself?
Do you head to the bar
to invest in a shot of whiskey?
No.
You buy coffee for your friend.

So when the Creator
gives Its precious currency
to buy a ticket home
on the Trans-universal Rocket
for you.
What do you buy?

Thank Your Barbells

It seems their only job is to thwart me:
the illness that shrivels my strength,
the neighbor whose threats time-travel me to my past,
where I once huddled shivering,
that job that presses like a relentless spring gale.

But when I call on the Shining One
I see...
a sublime life shaped by the pressure
of those very counterweights.

The illness teaches me to be honest.
The neighbor reminds me where love is.
The job transforms all work into service.

Like the weightlifter pressing barbells,
droplets of sweat form on the brow
as the muscles strengthen.

So when I aim to curse
the pain, frustration, boredom and despair,
I turn, and instead say,
Thank you!

Re-wild Your Life

After grey wolves were reintroduced into Yellowstone National Park in 1995, many things changed.

- The forests and meadows thrived in places where an over-abundance of deer had over-grazed them.
- Smaller animals such as beavers, otters, songbirds and hawks flourished in the newly fruitful ecosystem.
- And even the rivers changed course due to their shores being strengthened by plant growth.

Imagine what happens in our inner ecosystem when we reintroduce the power of the Omnipotent One, who was banished so long ago.

The Counter Force

Bless the mischief makers
who bring us to our knees.

Whether boss, neighbor, mate,
child or stranger,
they bully
trip
hound
and manipulate us.

They steal our money,
energy and time.

But most of all
they force us to fly into the flame
where we burn away
those parts of us
that they mirror.

Thus we live
in the full glory
of Love.

Warrior Marks

We stand like that tree
with lovers' hearts,
buddys' brands
and lone travelers' musings,
incised long ago
now distorted into burnt wounds.

Their original meaning buried
in the sap and bark of ages
and yet ready at any moment
to bleed across this now,
obscuring all truth.

Only the Omnipotent One
can turn these wounds
into warrior marks.
Only through that power
can we see the beauty
in our deformity.

As we stretch our branches
high into the limitless sky
the marks become kitten scratches
so far below,
then disappear completely
in the golden hue
of love.

Relish the Resistance

My palms press
against water
push through to my thighs
while my legs flutter.

I swim forward.

I don't try
to make the water disappear.
I don't want it
to drain away.

Instead I rejoice in the resistance
against my muscles
which strengthens them
with every pull
through the glistening ocean
of life.

Monsoon Lovemaking

You smell it on the breeze,
sweet scent of wet piñon and red dust
blowing off an advancing thunderhead.

When the towering anvil arrives
it casts bruised shadows,
pelts all with frozen rain
and thunders into your core.

You call on the Eternal One
hold steady through the storm.
Parched desert softens, convictions evaporate.

A bird chirps, and another...
You lift your head to realize
the relentless assault has stopped.

Birthed in its wake, a cool, moist breeze.
And the scent that teased you before
swirls in your being
like a love-drunk dervish.

The True Guide

I thought I knew the way
having traveled this path long ago
but no...I get lost in cryptic directions:
turn right at the big tree
left where the road forks.

All becomes muddled in duality.

"I don't know where I'm going
and I don't know how to get there!"

The Wayshower whispers:
"Surrender all thought,
all maps and scribbled directions."

When I do,
and suddenly come into the now,
I let this moment take me
through orchards and sunflower fields
under great oak arches
and over rickety bridges
across daunting chasms.

To my true home.
This mind that has been such a reliable frenemy must yield leadership to the one true Guide.

Feed the Torrent

On this drought day
when you ache for a gushing thunderstorm
yet only a spritz of rain cools your skin,
do not lose heart, my love.

The monsoon season's
splattering rain today
feeds the great torrent of tomorrow.

So one day when you hardly expect it
a billowing thunderhead will perch above you
and shower its manna
as you dance and twirl
naked in muddy puddles.

Remember Me

My memory is for my Beloved.
Mind wants to use it to...
ride the merry-go-round of the past,
dwell on playground kisses and slaps,
count my Monopoly money.

Actually...
If memory were a book
each page would only contain Your image.

If memory were a movie
every frame would be filled with Your ardor.

If memory were a song
every note would sing Your vibration.

I use memory to create my way into the higher worlds.

In Your image the past and future merge.

I remember You
in order to image the glory to come.
That glory is me.

Claim Your Playground

The lizard lifts high on his legs
and sprints alongside your bike.
His pointed nose and yellow stripes blur,
as he churns up the dust.

The raven swoops low
over your shoulder.
Her wings say whoosh, whoosh
as she breaks open the sky.

The water strider
skates on an invisible membrane.
His Martian shadow
dances among stones.

The wild lilac
bobs in the breeze.
Her sweet scent lures all
into her fragrant realm.

In every moment
the Beloved's souls
as they run, fly,
dance and infuse,
invite us to play.

But the mind sits
by the chain-link fence,
arms crossed,
mouth a jagged crease,
claiming dominion
over the playground.

You believe it,
and believe it,
until one day
a butterfly lands on your shoulder,
flutters her wings
and lifts you an inch off the ground.

With no hesitation,
you claim the playground,
right now,
the whole damn thing,
as your own.

Rough Rider

How would I ever get home
if not for this road
with all its potholes?

Cure the Past

Out of seemingly nowhere
it comes
a dust devil racing across the desert
swirling up an image
from a week, a month—
ten, twenty, thirty years ago.

It's suddenly alive, a fighting bull breathing fire:
the thing your mate or child or mother said or did
or didn't say or do
that knocked you to the floor
and stomped on your heart.

It's true, real, vivid as a high-definition movie
with a bombastic soundtrack—
a heart surgeon's knife
poised to cut deep.

And it does cut, only with yet more pain
because the incision point is already an old, old scar,
or many scars, ones you don't even remember,
maybe even from another life!

This time, however, you're armed.
You remember that *all* is exalted.
All is love!

That ancient or recent word or deed
churning within the mind
was not from the husband, wife, sister or child.

It was a love poem from the Friend to call you back,
to remind you that you are not that mate, daughter,
writer or neighbor
but are instead
a whirling universe:
infinite
eternal
free.

part III

an invitation to fly – transformation

Half Moon Dances

Half-moon dances
with pink cloud
just as I dance with You.

So ephemeral these bodies
whether of stardust or mist.
We waltz and twirl beyond them
into the realm of eternal bliss.

An Invitation to Fly

That challenge you face today
with your mate or employer,
your bank account or health,
it is an egg.

It's not just part of an omelet, though,
or a scramble with onions and peppers.

It is more like a finch or hummingbird egg.
One day the chick will peck its way free
and learn to fly.

It will lay an egg or two
and birth even more chirping glory.

This bird may pollinate plants,
add nutrients to the soil,
and carry seeds to distant lands.
Those seeds will grow into towering trees
where other birds can perch.

And one day a little girl may lift her eyes to the sky,
see one of those birds soar from a branch,
and realize her own possibility for infinite flight.

So the next time a challenge knocks at your door,
and in desperation you call on the Beloved for help,
open the door wide—
it is an invitation to fly.

The Seduction

You walk along the road,
sun warm on your cheeks
love sparkling in your eyes
as you know where you're going.

From a side street that handsome one
with chocolate brown eyes
and lips made for kissing
gestures you over,
envelops you in a hug.

This is the love you've been waiting for!

You make plans for the future,
reminisce about the past.

He tells you you're beautiful
and then every time you pass a mirror
you check to see if maybe he is right.

As the days pass, your fingers intertwined with his,
the sun that so warmed you from within,
instead begins to shine from him.

You dance to his music now late into the night,
your legs weak the next day, attention scattered.

But now all you have to do is please him
and the sun shines on you again.

Occasionally, at dawn,
you remember that road you were walking before...
that sense of direction you had.

But this, this is so easy!

Until that day when his eyes stray to another—
younger, prettier, new...

In that instant, the brilliant light extinguishes—
no warmth anywhere.
And you find yourself stumbling.
You bump your knees on furniture,
and your head reels in confusion.

You wilt in the darkness
and squirm a whole night in bed,
while pain contracts your heart
squeezing tears from your eyes.

Finally, you call out to the True Lover.

As a pink sun rises, you remember,
yes, you remember
the true sun within, always shining.

It's not necessary to please, to check the mirror,
to dance later than is good for you.
You can be honest, say what you need.
The handsome one may stay or go.
He can still hug you,
and even tell you you're pretty.

But now, you're back on the road
lit with your own Radiance.

Walk on the Wildflower Side

In this tavern, we drink honeysuckle nectar.
We stumble next door to the brothel, where
immaculate sex leaves us breathless.
Spent, we feast on a buffet of wispy clouds, sunrays
and moonbeams.
We mainline true ecstasy, leave all attachments
behind
and hitchhike across the Universe.
We dive from sheer cliffs into the Ocean of Love and
Mercy.
When we're with the real Intoxicator, we go wild—
inside!

The Call

It calls as though from a great distance
light years and galaxies away.
It whispers, quiet as the rustle of raven wings,
"Come."

And when I listen yet more closely
It explains how.
Between thoughts arrives a map
and a compass needle pointing home.

"Follow the beating pulse of your joy
the arc of your smile
the lilt of your laughter.
Follow as though they are the only realities.

"Simply wave to those hitch-hikers, Heartache and Pain
until they disappear in your rearview mirror.
Bypass that bleak ville, Despair, with its tumbleweed memories
and Resentment Saloon.

"Stop only when you reach Eternal Bliss,
that still pool of clear blue water."

Who are you? I ask.
How can I trust you? I plead.

With the harmony of a symphony
the voice replies
"I am you."

Sweet Intoxication

What if I call pain's bluff?
What if I look it in the eye and say
I am not afraid of you?

Do what you will.
You are only pain.
You cannot harm me, nor kill me.

For I am not this body with its
pinches, burns and aches;
the emotions with their
sadness, anxieties and rages;
the mind with its
frustrations, conundrums and confusions.

I am the momentum of the wave
conjured by a whale's fin.

I am the resonance of the mourning dove's coo.

I am the hangover from the lilac's sweet intoxication.

I am nothing and everything,
untouchable, unstoppable.
love.

The Clear Road Home

We have an easement
through these lower worlds
to our home.

But we must claim
our rite of passage.

We must maintain this inner road,
protect it from erosion
and false demands.

That surly neighbor
may try to block access,
but remember
the Beloved grants free passage.

Any moment we love that Power,
the way becomes clear.

Road Tripping into the Higher Worlds

Sometimes I scream in the dark
when my headlights aren't bright enough
to light the way.

Or in the daytime,
the icy rain
tight curves
road blocks
endless construction
and fog
thwart me.

I call out to You
and with Your love,
the obstacles diminish
and the mist clears.

Now I can see the horizon,
studded with sandstone mittens
and granite ships;
the valley of gilded cottonwoods
rimming the Rio Grande;
the red tail hawk
perched on a fencepost;
and the pronghorn
churning dust on the prairie.

With the pavement threading out to infinity,
white dashes disappearing beneath the hood
and this full tank of gas,
I know I can go anywhere.

The Wrinkle Road

My wrinkles are the roads
I have wandered in this life,
the paths up mountains
and through valleys.

This body,
one mere day hike
in the great landscape of eternity.

Eternal Spring

On a frigid winter night
when even icicles lose their grip
and clunk on the ground below,
the mind says "Wait, wait,
just a little longer
until the days lengthen.
Then the world will be brighter."

The Supreme answers, "Now, now,
this moment stretches to eternity.
Close your eyes
and bask in my sunshine.

"Inside, your tulips already blossom.
Your hyacinths and daffodils burst forth with delight.
Whenever you wait for spring
you leave me and enter the eternal winter
where my rays cannot caress you.

"Throw open your door
run naked through the piñon forest.
Let me warm you
until you realize your own Radiance."

Rogue River

I can't stop myself
from singing Your love.
It radiates from
my every pore.
Gag me, bind me,
lock me in a cell.
It still flows,
like a rogue river
bursting onto shore.

The Moon Serenades the Sun

With every orbit
my love waxes for You.
The power of Your brilliance
awakens this dead rock.

In those times when I must go dark—
or hide behind our friend Earth
the longing fills my craters
my Plato, Copernicus, and Kepler, to the brim.

But when Your effulgence again shines
on my Sea of Nectar, of Vapours, and Clouds,
my Ocean of Storms—
I lose concern over their dry lifelessness
because I have You to ignite me.

As our love deepens, I see
that You are not separate from me.

Any moment, in darkness or light
with just one thought of You
I enter the glow of my full self.

You are me and I am You
folded together with all the stars of all the galaxies
that are and ever will be.

Your love is
me.

Open to All

It drifts in from the west
a cloud, dark and churning.

Sitting on a ridgetop,
we watch its drunken steps
as it careens toward us.

Do we hunker down?
Do we run for cover?

We stay still
trusting the promise
hidden within its vapor.

From my lips escapes a prayer:
Please protect us, Cherished One.

The cloud arrives,
biting wind and swirling snow.
The view of the Sandia and Ortiz Mountains,
and all other landmarks
replaced by shifting gray.

Cheeks burning,
wind whistling in my ears,
I hold tight to the rocks,
turn my face from the gale.

But suddenly I look
straight at the snowflakes
hurtling toward me,
and they sparkle
reflecting a sun I cannot see.

Thousands of shining souls
dance up and down,
rush forward and back.
A whole company of ballerinas
join and separate
in perfect choreography.

The wind calms.
The tail of the cloud
blows past.
A few sparkles
kick up their heels
in an encore
and then disappear,
leaving my heart full,
open to any and all
experiences that may come.

Asteroid of Love

Oh, blessed asteroid
hurtling toward Earth
please annihilate me.

Destroy the piranhas
that gnaw on my heart.
Obliterate the gnats
that buzz in my head.

"Really?" a voice within whispers.
"What if you simply surrender,
let go of the concerns
you hold so dear?"

I call out for help,
chant and sit with the pain
of loosening mind's grip
on its many Legos and Barbies.

Suddenly, the Divine's
asteroid of love
soars within me.

Understanding dawns,
while with a puff of Breath,
all heartache
is balmed to smithereens.

Cove of Love

She slouches her shoulders,
unconsciously protecting her heart
but it only creates an aching knot
near her scapula.

She knows it's futile,
that there is no protection out here
with waves crashing all about.
Just the slow grind
of pain chasing pleasure.

She sees that she must
swim into the only safe place,
beyond time and space,
that quiet cove of love.

And so she calls
to the Redeemer
the one sent
to guide her home.

In that Radiance, she knows—
no protection necessary
no slouching shoulders,
for all is an amorous ocean.

No harm, nor heartache
can come to the eternal one,
for all is she
and she is Thee.

part IV

sail the cosmic seas —
traveling the inner worlds

We Are Gypsies

The mind wants to know
where we're going,
what motel we'll sleep in tonight.
It wants to know
what diner we will eat at
and what's on the menu too.

But really, we are gypsies,
we are Bedouins
traveling the great distance,
each day a surprise oasis in the desert
a gift in its freshness,
its quenching depths.

Such uncertainty
makes imperative the Guide.
Following its precise compass
we relax and watch
the crystalline, snow-covered peaks
the daisies along the lane
and the shimmering blue of a promising sky,
all leading us home.

Hula of Love

Wildflower seed,
the sun's rays warm you
and the spark ignites within.

With exuberance,
you break free of the dark, crusty earth
and bloom.

As storm clouds rumble
and spring winds swirl
you bend and sway—
a hula of love.

Sail the Cosmic Seas

Out here
in the far reaches of creation,
I sail the Cosmic seas
between stars.

Like Voyager,
I swing past Jupiter,
frolic among Saturn's rings,
and discover Titan's thick blue haze.

Now, the One draws me back.
It tugs at my third eye
and whispers in my ear:
"Come home."

I am no one-way probe
destined to wander the Universe
for eternity.

Such a thing does not exist.
All returns to its origin—
eventually.

Like a child
back from summer camp
running toward her father's open arms,
I sprint homeward,
into the great love
that I am.

Born in Winter

If you were born and lived in eternal winter
you might believe that only gray skies and frozen
fields exist.
You might adapt and learn to love the shimmering
flesh of snow.
You might master the art of throwing snowballs
and appreciate sleeping long hours in abundant
darkness.

But you would not know the tender poppy blossoms
of spring,
the bone piercing heat of summer,
or the scarlet leaves of fall.

Truth is many seasons larger than the mind's
landscape.

Truth is certain that when one gives
one will always receive more.

When one dies,
one is born.

When one loves,
one knows God.

All I Ever Need to Be

The mountain does not try to be majestic.
It simply stands tall, letting the light and seasons
play across its shoulders.

The river does not force itself to flow faster.
It just follows its own frolicking meander
to the sea.

The sun does not compete with other stars in the
galaxy.
It merely shines its brilliance
upon all within reach.

All I ever need to be
I already am.

Love Hurricane

The tiniest flutter of your
butterfly wing
initiates a hurricane
of love.

Dance to the Song Within

A tap on my shoulder signals me to step into the center of a circle of revelers. This is a dance-off on an autumn Sunday night. A thin, bearded man has also been tagged and now stands in front of me. I start moving in an odd way, what feels like Elaine's notorious dance on *Seinfeld*. I've never been confident about the way I dance, but I still do it secretly in my great room to my favorite songs. Now I sway my hips and swirl my arms to the sound of techno jazz.

My partner seems relaxed. He lifts his legs and stomps his feet, vibrating his head so that the circle around us laughs. After he and I leave the center and tap the shoulders of two others, they start their dance. Watching them, and the circle of about ten people, I realize that the goal is to make people laugh.

My boyfriend, a tall, strong, German, enters the center with a sturdy woman wearing golden braids, and they spend their ten seconds shoving each other around and smashing their hips together, which causes major hilarity. Another woman lies down on the floor as in a break dance move, though she doesn't spin. A man jerks with robotic precision. My next turn, I revert to my childhood gymnastics and do a handstand, which draws a few "aahs" from the group.

I laugh along with them, but even though the air smells of apple crisp and red wine and the atmosphere feels jovial, I'm uncomfortable. There is something untrue about this that my mind wants to judge. These are my mate's friends. I know that *my* friends would never put on such an exhibition.

Later, thoughts swirl within me as I try to sleep in a queen bed with my boyfriend and his Dalmatian. It's as though that wild dancing is still happening within my chest. It thumps and jerks through the night. I wake exhausted.

Only during my morning spiritual practice, when I center my attention on my Beloved's writing, does clarity dawn.

The discomfort has nothing to do with the dance-off. It really was fun, and a beautiful expression of silly pleasure for our party hosts and their guests. As my Beloved says, "Nothing is unclean of itself." I'm just afraid that I'm not a funny dancer. And when I really look at this, I realize that it's okay. I don't have to be. I see how this experience reflects life. How often during our days are we tapped on the shoulder and asked to enter the game?

The usual response is just what mine was, to play for the crowd, to try to be pretty or smart, to please the boss or mate, to win the game, the move, or the love—to compete and try to be what we fear we are not.

I take a few moments to revise the night, to see myself doing it differently. What if, when tapped on the shoulder, I had felt the Ecstacy fill my heart and danced to that eternal, omnipotent, and stunning beat? I see my arms as great wings taking flight above any self-doubt and, my legs too, levitating into the sky. I float, flip, and twirl in the Essence, as though I were completely weightless, formless even, without a care to hold me down. That is the dance I can do in any and every moment when I surrender and disappear into the felicity of now.

Be

Be...
neither for nor against.

Just
love.

United by Our Essence

Oh virga, blue curtain in the sky
I envy you.
Suspended there in the glowing light,
never do you fall upon the ground,
swirl down the drain,
or lose yourself in a puddle.

Instead your icy tendrils
simply evaporate.

But I am a river
laboring across the contours of this rocky earth
as the sea pulls me home.

I stumble over rocks and smash into trees.
I'm stopped dead by dams
and tainted by mines.

But the Eternal One has graced me as well.

I glisten in the evening light,
gurgle through pebble pools
slake the thirst of deer and rabbits
stroke the fins of trout
and reflect back the image of all,
showing the world its beauty.

That includes you, dear virga.
With your luminosity shining upon me
I come to be my ethereal self.

And then I see
that we are not separate.

Our true essence:
Fluidity.

House Built of Kisses

We live in a house built of kisses,
each one bestowed by the True Lover's lips.

Whether health or sickness,
ultra-conservative or flaming liberal,
lilting flute or barking dog,
toxic swamp or crystalline lake,
all are essential to the whole abode
that coaxes and pushes us
to the inner-most home.

Here we realize
we are the Beloved's kiss—
and the kisser.

The Eternally Bright Day

That hurt that stops you like a bear trap,
metal teeth cutting to the bone
is but a raindrop on a hot rock.
It sizzles and then evaporates.

But the mind tells the story
of pain and blood, and a cold winter storm
until the hurt becomes a bomb
dropped on your city of life,
mushroom cloud dissipating all reason and love.

What if, instead, on this longest, darkest night,
in the knowingness of our eternity
we leave our backpack of hurt in the valley
and climb switchbacks with the Guide.

With this effervescence
we skip up the trail,
and suddenly *become* the mountain,
weighed only by wild raspberries
on spindly limbs.

We are also the valley below
stretching to the river
where fields of sunflowers
tango along the bank.

And we are the sun that shines above,
our invisible rays nourishing all
into existence.

The Mansion Within

It seems so solid,
this gingerbread house
with its cookie siding,
chocolate-wafer roof
and frosting adornments,
when really it is
only flour, butter, sugar and spice.

The walls we lean on
crumble away with the slightest pressure
or melt to mush in a glass of milk.

Meanwhile, the true mansion
stays steady within.
Its walls of humility
mortar of patience
floor of contentment
and roof of balance
never, ever succumb
to an emotional tornado
or mental wrecking ball.

Such assaults
simply move right through,
with no collision.

So enjoy the gingerbread house,
relish its sweetness and fun,
but light the evening fire
in your inner home with the Friend,
and sit peacefully in the warm glow.

The Radiant Poppy

Just now, under the frozen earth
the seed awakens.
Its heart begins a faint thump, thump,
and its tiny hands tucked in tight
tremble with a life
ready to burst forth in spring.

So do I, kissed by a warming Sun
feel the pulse of new energy beat within.

What do I do with this love?

Each moment I decide:
Will I be a weed growing goat-head fruit
that pricks the passerby?
Or am I a poppy with its capacity for delight
and its glowing orange petals
that make even the grumpy horned toad smile?

This awakening moment, this now,
determines what sprouts
and grows.

The Stray Dog

The dog you rescued
with a scar on her brow
wags her tail
and looks up at you,
dark eyes shining
mouth curved in a little smile.

But that lonely road
where you found her limping
stays branded on her heart.

In a tough moment,
as she huddles in the corner
wrapped in fear,
you scratch her ears
and tell her she's safe.

She's remembering some hostile kick
or maybe the bump from a car
that broke her hip,
which never fully healed.

The only way to help her
is to comfort her
as those old images play out,
so she can trust this moment,
and live fearlessly.

And so in every possible way
you show her those days are past.
She lives in a new place now:
a home with a cushion to sleep on,
(or really the bed and couch)
healthy food at mealtime
and beef bones from the butcher.

In the night
she snuggles against your body
her paws jiggling
as she chases butterflies
through a wildflower meadow,
a glimpse of the freedom
she truly is.

Love Eclipses All

Like lovers attracted
by forces beyond their control
the sun and moon
magnetize.

As they merge,
the dusky moon
overlaps the persimmon sun—
a bite from an apple.

Then darkness—
all goes quiet,
the robins silent
the squirrels still.

Totality.

The corona appears,
rainbow edges
and a golden, radiant
halo.

Time Travel

If I could travel back
to that moment
when I accepted that seducer's invitation
and instead simply say,
"No thank you,"
saving me a world of hurt...

If I could go back
to that dinner in Africa
and not eat that amoeba
that stayed in my belly,
stealing my strength for decades...

If I could stop that car
from killing my sister,
or take my mother to the hospital sooner
so the doctor could fight
the pneumonia in time...

Would I?

Of course, I can revise my past actions in any now,
but what if I could also change the outcomes?

Mind swoons with the notion:
Maybe life would be lighter, easier.
I would be steadier, healthier,
less plagued by stress and fear.

But then...
I may not have met the Friend.

Inside, I ask...what is the truth?

The answer comes in a shower of love:
All the past is crucial,
none of it important.

An eye blink
in a lifetime of seeing.

A firefly's flash
among all the stars in the Milky Way.

A dew drop
on an orchid petal in a rainforest.

Instead of time-traveling back,
I journey inward now,
where all disappears
into the golden hue of You.

part V

wag your tail – service

The Full Life of a Dew Drop

The dew drop forms
on a pear blossom
glistens in first light
trembles in a breeze
slips onto a lizard tongue
and loses itself
in giving.

Purrfect Love

I hold my cat, Arjuna, in my lap
pry open her mouth.
She jerks away
and races around the house.

"I will not hurt you," I plead.
"It is medicine to make you well."

I see the reflection:
Each day, the True Physician
pries open the clenched jaws
of mind's stolid ways.

After I squirt the antibiotic
in her mouth,
Arjuna, betrayed,
hides in the shadows.

But later, during the quiet
of my spiritual practice
she returns,
curls up in my lap
and remains still as I.

We commune in the quiet,
soak in the Love
purr together as One.

Love Allows

The Beloved allows us to be.
No pushing, no force,
those are of the mind.
The divine Power offers all with an open palm,
encourages us to unwrap the next gift
but with no pressure.

As the Beloved of my microcosm
I can do so as well.
I can allow these lower bodies
physical, emotional, mental,
to be what they are,
not trying to force
them into a new state.

And I can allow the same
with the blessed souls who
surround me.
I let them be
while I commune
with the Sound.

I step in when necessary,
nurture, love,
but no pushing or force.
All will come along
in their own perfect time.

Morning Song

The music of morning:
chirp chirp, cluck
whoee whoee
slip slip
yee yee yee
woo wit woo wit.

A waning moon glows
against the pale rosy sky
drip drip of dew
breeze wraps like a cool cloak.

Thump, thump, thump...
My heart plays the percussion
of this love symphony
amplifying it
throughout the Cosmos.

Shifting Tides

The moon observes
the shifting tides
high, low
through day and night
fazed not
but fully aware
that all responds
to its gravity.

Love with Impunity

Tentative love, like a bubble
blown through a child's wand.
Pop, and it disappears.

All the daisy petals fall
with a single uttering of
"He loves me not."

But really, love, LOVE, is more like air,
always present.
The more one exhales
the more rushes in to fill our lungs.

It is like the ocean
whose tides never cease
dancing with the moon.

Like the hummingbird's wings
that flap with such fury
you can't even see them.

So give up this crazy idea
of love as a dissolving mist.
Love with impunity!

Love like that rescue mutt
who never leaves his master's heels.
Love like that sacred mesa
that hugs the earth,
with unshakable constancy.

Know that all the love played on Your flute
echoes back as a symphony.

The Jurassic Scream

My lover says his head, cheek and teeth sear with lightning pain.
Immediately mind kicks in—must help, must find a cure.

Ask Siri, query Alexa, Google it, Bing it, WebMD it—
that place where the common cold becomes a life-threatening illness.

Acupuncture, Ayurveda, Reiki...
A diet—there must be a diet for this!

Isn't there a diet to cure everything?
Even to get to heaven?

I stop, breathless, call on the Genuine Healer.

Truth enters in a rush of love:
What if this condition is my loved one's perfect teaching?
What if it is not mine to cure?

What if I recognize the sacredness of my own
journey
and keep my attention there?

I can support him, love him.
But most of all...
Let him have his invaluable experience.

What if I had never trudged through the jungle of
my own pain,
cried out like a howler monkey in the night
that Jurassic scream that reminds me to desire only
You?

To wake in the morning strong and healthy is a gift.

To live every moment beyond any lower concern—
pure freedom.

What If?

What if I can be love
no matter what's going on
in my physical body,
with my house
or in the world?

This is the Exalted One's promise:

Whenever I put my attention
on that Power,
I am.

The Winning Hand

In a smoky room
scented with bourbon and sweat
I clasp my cards so tightly
they bend.

This hand with its
hearts, clubs, and diamonds
is everything.

Whether good or bad,
I bet on it
believing the win or loss
depends on the deal.

Finally, bereft,
my chips gone
my account indebted
I call out for help,
and see . . .
the Divine hand
trumps all!

It is the royal flush,
the real amidst illusion.

Whether I hold
a full house
or a pair of twos
when I show the True Dealer's hand
the air clears to a shimmering stillness
and the whole game folds
into the oneness of love.

Ode to Cilantro

Oh Cilantro, most benign of herbs,
why do so many despise you?

Even Rosemary, with her piney sharpness,
doesn't endure such scorn.

And Thyme, with all his pungency,
fields little grief.

Meanwhile Sage, exuding bitterness,
rarely invokes a complaint.

And of course,
everyone loves that Sweet Basil.

While your cousin Parsley, with all its curls,
is invited to every party!

But you, Cilantro,
who chefs casually toss onto tacos and stir-fries,
ignite the scorn of even Julia Child,
who claimed she would pluck you from a dish
and cast you to the floor.

Cilantrophobes say you taste like soap,
but if they could only give you a chance,
let their minds rewire to accept you,
they might savor your humility.

A bit sweet and quite earthy,
you bring flavors together
with no need to stand out,
or scream across a plate.

Like the one who holds open the door
for all to pass in before her,
you allow the food to be first,
while adding a touch of green
and a little zing.

Melt into Love

The temperature warms.
The ice melts.
So does the frozen heart
in the presence of the Friend.

Spring Is Here!

One cannot rush winter.
One cannot make the earth warm,
the buds blossom,
the rain fall.

Each experience inhales and exhales
its own perfect breath,
the lessons tucked within the moonless nights
and pelting corn snow.

Why wait?
Why hope for the future?
Spring is already here!

In this moment
the sun shines golden within.
The robins chirp
and the morning glories burst forth.

All with one glance
into the Cherished One's eyes.

The Old Lover

The old lover,
handsome in that rugged way,
swaggers to your table
holds out his hand
and asks for a dance.

You know you can follow
that ancient desire
into his arms
two-step across the scuffed wood floor
intoxicated by his mind-fogging cologne.

But then you remember
how, in his carelessness,
he stepped on your toes,
aggressively twirled you,
and flung you across the room.

You recall that jittery discomfort
the excitement-hangover the next day,
and the remorse
for slamming into others.

So instead you call on the True Dancer,
smile and decline the offer.
You move inside to the comforting arms
and waltz in the smooth, floating glory
of love.

Invest in Me

I put money in real estate,
in the stock market,
in that high-yield CD.
Goosebumps pimple the skin.
How much will I make?
the mind wonders.

The balance rises
as I count the riches,
a warm blanket of safety
across my life.

But then...always
the condo sits vacant,
the Dow tumbles,
I need cash and it's tied up
in that darn CD.

I listen as the true Financial Advisor says,
Only one investment
offers safety now and forever.
Only one investment
pays limitless dividends

and eternally compounded interest.
Only one investment
is worth the effort.

All else is effect.

Invest in Me
that inner Power says
and all will come to you.

The True Ruler

You are the true ruler of the only free world,
elected every moment you enter the now.

Imbibe in the Omnipotent One's power and grace within,
and then lead wisely.

Instill each second with the
generosity of the sun
giving its warmth without expectation;
the harmony of the planets,
each one unique while orbiting together;
and the love of the entire universe,
here to compel us inward.

Nothing can ever harm your kingdom
when the True Ruler takes the throne.

Become Hopeless

Give up hope
for better health
for peace with your neighbor
for a lasting relationship.

Trade in that tinsel
for actual gold.

Mind says, "No!"

"If I lose hope
I have nothing left in my pockets.

"Without hope,
the Grand Canyon yawns in my heart."

Exactly!

Nothing on low to scheme about,
to focus on,
to try for.

No thing!

When you quit hoping the rain will stop
you pull out your umbrella.

In this hope-less vacuum
floating free of gravity,
all one can do is love.

When all that's left is love,
all that remains
is the true self.

My Perfect Teaching

The pain in my stomach,
the wrangling with my neighbor,
the bills,
the restless winter nights,
these are the water
through which I learn to swim.

"Can't I just stand on shore
while you teach me?"
the mind pleads.

"No."

I dive in
so the Sacred One can show me
how easily I float.

Once in the water, I grasp...
it is all for me.
The breast and backstroke,
crawl and butterfly
are the manna of soul,
and the water merely
the resistant force.

Soon that tsunami turns placid
and I soar weightless,
do somersaults and handstands
relish the bubbles tingling on my skin.

This ocean is my perfect teaching
and You,
my sublime swimming Master.

Death by Selfie

She stands with her back to the cliff edge
camera poised arm's length
capturing the indigo sky and craggy canyon below.

Moving her head into the frame,
she poses just right
eyes wide to disguise an intruding brow,
daring smile to impress her friends.

She tilts the camera to capture more,
inches back
and back yet farther.

A pebble shifts beneath her foot
and she slips...
plunging into the abyss.

As she falls,
she sees her folly, over-valuing this outer shell.
She calls out to the Humble One.

That Power catches her
in an open palm
and delivers her back to her true
self.

Wag Your Tail

Be a service dog for consciousness
shepherding patience into the world.
Lie at your master's feet
awaiting its direction
panting for its every whim.

Walk with that Power
alert for moments to aid
with your simple presence
the sick
the hungry
the empty hearts
the lost souls wandering like zombies
life's endless cul-de-sac.

One lick of your tongue
brightens the whole Universe!

The service dog never whines,
never says "This is too much—
I must escape this master!"

No
The service dog wags its tail
eager to love.

About the Author

From a young age I began using writing as a way to explore my inner experiences. Since I grew up on a ranch in northern New Mexico, I also was connected to nature. The two passions have woven the fabric of my life. In college, I majored in journalism, and in graduate school, I received an MFA in creative writing. For eight years I taught college English, until I found the courage to begin writing professionally. My career quickly gathered momentum, and soon I was writing for *The New York Times*, the Frommer's and Dummies travel guides, *Audubon* magazine, and United Airlines *Hemispheres Magazine*, among others. For eight years I wrote, photographed, and videotaped stories for my King of the Road column in *New Mexico Magazine*. In 1997, I came under the tutelage of spiritual Master Sri Gary Olsen. Since then I have devoted my life and writing to the inner journey. I am author of a memoir, *All In for Love*, a novel, *The Baby Pact*, and I blog at *The Inner Adventure*.

www.lesleysking.com

www.ingramcontent.com/pod-product-compliance
Lightning Source LLC
Chambersburg PA
CBHW070550050426
42450CB00011B/2792